Words

Copyright © 1974 Lion Publishing

Published by
Lion Publishing plc
Sandy Lane West, Oxford, England
ISBN 0 7459 1968 5 (paperback)
ISBN 0 7459 2102 7 (cased)
Albatross Books Pty Ltd
PO Box 320, Sutherland, NSW 2232, Australia
ISBN 0 7324 0252 2 (paperback)
ISBN 0 7324 0459 2 (cased)

First edition in this format 1991

Photographs by Patricia and Charles Aithie - ffotograff.
Additional photographs by Tino Qahoush: pages 19, 29, 39.

Quotations from *Good News Bible*, copyright 1966, 1971 and 1976 American
Bible Society; published by the Bible Societies and Collins.

Printed and bound in Singapore

◆ *Words of* ◆
THANKS

A LION BOOK
Oxford · Batavia · Sydney

✦ THANK YOU, LORD ✦

I thank you, Lord, with all my heart;
    I sing praise to you before the gods.
I bow down in front of your holy temple and praise
    your name,
because of your constant love and faithfulness,
    because you have shown that you and your
    commands are supreme.
You answered me when I called to you;
    with your strength you strengthened me.

All the kings of the earth will praise you, Lord,
    because they have heard your promises.
They will sing about what the Lord has done,
    and about his great glory.
Even though the Lord is so high above,
    he cares for the lowly
    and the proud cannot hide from him.

From PSALM 138

◆ FAITHFUL AND JUST ◆

Praise the Lord!

With all my heart I will thank the Lord,
    in the meeting of his people.
How wonderful are the things the Lord does!
    All who are pleased with them want to understand
    them.
All he does is full of honour and majesty;
    his righteousness is eternal...

In all he does he is faithful and just;
    all his commandments are dependable.
They last for all time;
    they were given in truth and righteousness.
He brought salvation to his people,
    and made an eternal covenant with them.
    Holy and mighty is he!
The way to become wise is to fear the Lord;
    he gives sound judgement to all who obey his
    commands.
He is to be praised for ever!

From PSALM 111

◆ AS LONG AS I LIVE ◆

Praise the Lord!
   Praise the Lord, my soul!
I will praise him as long as I live;
   I will sing to my God all my life.

Don't put your trust in human leaders,
   or anyone else who cannot save you.
When they die they return to the soil;
   on that day all their plans come to an end...

The Lord sets prisoners free
   and gives sight to the blind.
He raises all who are humbled;
   he loves his righteous people.
He protects the foreigners who live in the land;
   he helps widows and orphans,
      but ruins the plans of the wicked...

The Lord will be king for ever!
   Your God, Zion, will reign for all time!

Praise the Lord!

From PSALM 146

• HE GIVES ANIMALS •
THEIR FOOD...

Praise the Lord!

It is good to sing praise to our God;
    it is pleasant and right to praise him...

He has determined the number of the stars
    and calls each one by name.
Great and almighty is our Lord;
    his knowledge cannot be measured.
He raises the humble,
    but crushes the wicked to the ground.
Sing hymns of praise to the Lord;
    play music to our God on the harp.
He spreads clouds over the sky;
    he provides rain for the earth,
    and makes grass grow on the hills.
He gives animals their food,
    and feeds the young ravens when they call...

He takes pleasure in those who fear him,
    in those who trust in his constant love...

Praise the Lord!

From PSALM 147

✦ MY SAVIOUR ✦

How I love you, Lord!
    You are my defender.
The Lord is my Saviour;
    he is my strong fortress.
My God is my protection,
    and I am safe with him.
He protects me like a shield;
    he defends me and keeps me safe.
I call to the Lord,
    and he saves me from my enemies.
Praise the Lord!

From PSALM 18

◆ GOD'S FLOCK ◆

Come, let us praise the Lord!
    Let us sing for joy to our protector and Saviour!
Let us come before him with thanksgiving,
    and sing joyful songs of praise!
For the Lord is a mighty God,
    a mighty king over all the gods.
He rules over the whole earth,
    from the deepest caves to the highest hills.
He rules over the sea, which he made;
    the land also, which he himself formed.

Come, let us bow down and worship him;
    let us kneel before the Lord, our Maker!
He is our God;
    we are the people he looks after,
    the flock for which he provides.

From PSALM 95

✦ GOD HAS HELPED ME ✦

Give praise to the Lord;
    he has heard my cry for help!
The Lord protects and defends me;
    I trust in him.
He has helped me, and so I am glad
    and sing hymns of praise to him.

The Lord protects his people;
    he defends and saves his chosen king.
Save your people, Lord,
    and bless those who are yours!
Be their shepherd,
    and take care of them for ever.

From PSALM 28

◆ THIRST WILL BE SATISFIED ◆

God, you are my God,
   and I long for you.
My whole being desires you;
   my soul is thirsty for you,
   like a dry, worn-out, and waterless land.
Let me see you in the sanctuary;
   let me see how mighty and glorious you are.
Your constant love is better than life itself,
   and so I will praise you.
I will give thanks to you as long as I live;
   I will raise my hands to you in prayer.
My soul will feast and be satisfied
   and I will sing glad songs of praise to you.

From PSALM 63

✦ HOW GOOD THE LORD IS ✦

I will always thank the Lord;
    I will never stop praising him.
I will praise him for what he has done;
    may all who are oppressed listen and be glad!
Proclaim with me the Lord's greatness;
    let us praise his name together!

I prayed to the Lord, and he answered me;
    he freed me from all my fears.
The oppressed look to him and are glad;
    they will never be disappointed.
The helpless call to him, and he answers;
    he saves them from all their troubles.
His angel guards those who fear the Lord
    and rescues them from danger.

Find out for yourself how good the Lord is!
    Happy is the man who finds safety with him!
Fear the Lord, all his people;
    those who fear him have all they need.
Even lions lack food and go hungry,
    but those who obey the Lord lack nothing good.

From PSALM 34

◆ ALL NATIONS, ALL PEOPLES ◆

Praise the Lord, all nations!
    Praise him, all peoples!
His constant love for us is strong,
    and his faithfulness is eternal.

Praise the Lord!

PSALM 117

◆ GOD SAVES ◆

I waited and waited for the Lord's help;
    then he listened to me and heard my cry.
He pulled me out of a dangerous pit,
    out of a muddy hole!
He set me safely on a rock
    and made me secure.
He taught me to sing a new song,
    a song of praise to our God.
Many who see this will be afraid
    and will put their trust in the Lord...

Lord, I know you will never stop being
    merciful to me!
Your love and loyalty will always keep
    me safe.

From PSALM 40

✦ GOD CARES ✦

Praise the Lord!

You servants of the Lord,
    praise his name!
His name will be praised,
    now and for ever!
From the east to the west,
    the Lord's name be praised!
The Lord rules over all nations,
    his glory is above the heavens.

There is no one like the Lord our God;
he lives in the heights above,
    but he bends down
    to see the heavens and the earth.
He raises the poor from the dust;
    he lifts the needy from their misery,
and makes them companions of princes,
    the princes of his people.
He honours the childless wife in her home;
    he makes her happy by giving her children.

Praise the Lord!

PSALM 113

◆ ALL LIVING THINGS ◆

The Lord is faithful to his promises,
    and good in all he does.
He helps all who are in trouble;
    he raises all who are humbled.
All living things look hopefully to him,
    and he gives them food when they need it.
He gives them enough
    and satisfies the needs of all.
The Lord is righteous in all he does,
    merciful in all his acts.
He is near to all who call to him,
    who call to him with sincerity.
He supplies the needs of all who fear him;
    he hears their cry and saves them.
He protects all who love him,
    but he will destroy all the wicked.
I will always praise the Lord;
    let all creatures praise his holy name for
    ever!

From PSALM 145

◆ PRAISE THE LORD, ◆
MY SOUL!

Praise the Lord, my soul!
   All my being, praise his holy name!
Praise the Lord, my soul,
   and do not forget how kind he is.
He forgives all my sins
   and heals all my diseases;
he saves me from the grave
   and blesses me with love and mercy;
he fills my life with good things,
   so that I stay young and strong like an eagle...

The Lord set up his throne in heaven;
   he is king over all.
Praise the Lord, you strong and mighty angels,
   who obey his commands,
   who listen to what he says!
Praise the Lord, all you heavenly powers,
   you servants who do what he wants!
Praise the Lord, all his creatures,
   in every place he rules!
Praise the Lord, my soul!

From PSALM 103

✦ HOW GREAT YOU ARE ✦

We praise you, God, we praise you!
We proclaim how great you are,
and tell the wonderful things you have done!...

Judgement does not come from the east or from the
    west, from the north or from the south;
it is God who does the judging,
    putting some down and lifting others up.
The Lord holds a cup in his hand,
    full of fresh wine, very strong;
he pours it out, and all the wicked drink it;
    they drink it down to the last drop.

But I will never stop speaking of the God of Jacob,
    or singing praises to him.
He will break the power of the wicked,
    but the power of the righteous will be increased.

From PSALM 75

◆ WHY AM I TROUBLED? ◆

Send your light and your truth;
    may they lead me and bring me
    back to Zion, your sacred hill,
    and to your temple, where you live!
Then I will go to your altar, God,
    because you give me joy and happiness;
I will play my harp and sing praise to you,
    God, my God!

Why am I sad?
    Why am I troubled?
I will put my hope in God,
    and once again I will praise him,
    my Saviour and my God.

From PSALM 43

♦ THE GOD OF HISTORY ♦

Give thanks to the Lord, proclaim his greatness,
    and make known to the nations what he has done!
Sing to him, sing praise to him;
    tell all the wonderful things he has done!
Be glad that we belong to him;
    let all who serve the Lord rejoice!
Go to the Lord for help;
    stay in his presence always.
You descendants of Abraham, his servant,
    you descendants of Jacob, his chosen one;
remember his great and wonderful miracles,
    and the judgements he gave...

Praise the Lord!

From PSALM 105

✦ THIS GOD IS OUR GOD ✦

Inside your temple, God,
    we think of your constant love.
You are praised by people everywhere,
    and your fame extends over all the earth.
You rule with justice;
    let the people of Zion be glad!
You give right judgements;
    let there be joy in the cities of Judah!

Walk all round Mount Zion and count its towers,
    take notice of its walls, and examine its fortresses,
so that you may tell the next generation
    that this God is our God, for ever and ever;
    he will lead us for all time to come.

From PSALM 48

◆ PRAISE HIM WITH ◆ TRUMPETS

Praise the Lord!

Praise God in his temple!
    Praise his strength in heaven!
Praise him for the mighty things he has done!
    Praise his supreme greatness!

Praise him with trumpets!
    Praise him with harps and lyres!
Praise him with drums and dancing!
    Praise him with harps and flutes!
Praise him with cymbals!
    Praise him with loud cymbals!
Praise the Lord, all living creatures!

Praise the Lord!

PSALM 150

◆ PRAISE HIM, ALL THAT ◆
HE HAS MADE

Praise the Lord!

Praise him, sun and moon;
    praise him, shining stars!
Praise him, highest heavens,
    and the waters above the sky!...

Praise the Lord from the earth,
    sea monsters and all ocean depths;
lightning and hail, snow and clouds,
    strong winds that obey his command!

Praise him, hills and mountains,
    fruit trees and forests;
all animals, tame and wild,
    reptiles and birds!

Praise him, kings and all peoples,
    princes and all other rulers;
young men and girls,
    old people and children also!

Let them all praise the name of the Lord...

Praise the Lord!

From PSALM 148